BIRD PARLIAMENT

Farid ud-Din Attar

BIRD PARLIAMENT

Translated by
EDWARD FITZGERALD

BIBLIOBAZAAR

BIRD PARLIAMENT

BIRD PARLIAMENT

Once on a time from all the Circles seven
Between the stedfast Earth and rolling Heaven
THE BIRDS, of all Note, Plumage, and Degree,
That float in Air, and roost upon the Tree;
And they that from the Waters snatch their Meat,
And they that scour the Desert with long Feet;
Birds of all Natures, known or not to Man,
Flock'd from all Quarters into full Divan,
On no less solemn business than to find
Or choose, a Sultan Khalif of their kind,
For whom, if never theirs, or lost, they pined.
The Snake had his, 'twas said; and so the Beast
His Lion-lord: and Man had his, at least:
And that the Birds, who nearest were the Skies,
And went apparell'd in its Angel Dyes,
Should be without—under no better Law
Than that which lost all other in the Maw—
Disperst without a Bond of Union—nay,
Or meeting to make each the other's Prey—
This was the Grievance—this the solemn Thing
On which the scatter'd Commonwealth of Wing,
From all the four Winds, flying like to Cloud
That met and blacken'd Heav'n, and Thunder-loud
With Sound of whirring Wings and Beaks that clash'd
Down like a Torrent on the Desert dash'd:

Till by Degrees, the Hubbub and Pell-mell
Into some Order and Precedence fell,
And, Proclamation made of Silence, each
In special Accent, but in general Speech
That all should understand, as seem'd him best,
The Congregation of all Wings addrest.

And first, with Heart so full as from his Eyes
Ran weeping, up rose Tajidar the Wise;
The mystic Mark upon whose Bosom show'd
That He alone of all the Birds THE ROAD
Had travell'd: and the Crown upon his Head
Had reach'd the Goal; and He stood forth and said:

'O Birds, by what Authority divine
I speak you know by *His* authentic Sign,
And Name, emblazon'd on my Breast and Bill:
Whose Counsel I assist at, and fulfil:
At His Behest I measured as he plann'd
The Spaces of the Air and Sea and Land;
I gauged the secret sources of the Springs
From Cloud to Fish: the Shadow of my Wings
Dream'd over sleeping Deluge: piloted
The Blast that bore Sulayman's Throne: and led
The Cloud of Birds that canopied his Head;
Whose Word I brought to Balkis: and I shared
The Counsel that with Asaf he prepared.
And now you want a Khalif: and I know
Him, and his whereabout, and How to go:
And go alone I could, and plead your cause
Alone for all: but, by the eternal laws,
Yourselves by Toil and Travel of your own

Must for your old Delinquency atone.
Were you indeed not blinded by the Curse
Of Self-exile, that still grows worse and worse,
Yourselves would know that, though *you* see him not,
He is with you this Moment, on this Spot,
Your Lord through all Forgetfulness and Crime,
Here, There, and Everywhere, and through all Time.
But as a Father, whom some wayward Child
By sinful Self-will has unreconciled,
Waits till the sullen Reprobate at cost
Of long Repentance should regain the Lost;
Therefore, yourselves to see as you are seen,
Yourselves must bridge the Gulf you made between
By such a Search and Travel to be gone
Up to the mighty mountain Kaf, whereon
Hinges the World, and round about whose Knees
Into one Ocean mingle the Sev'n Seas;
In whose impenetrable Forest-folds
Of Light and Dark "Symurgh" his Presence holds;
Not to be reach'd, if to be reach'd at all
But by a Road the stoutest might apal;
Of Travel not of Days or Months, but Years—
Life-long perhaps: of Dangers, Doubts, and Fears
As yet unheard of: Sweat of Blood and Brain
Interminable—often all in vain—
And, if successful, no Return again:
A Road whose very Preparation scared
The Traveller who yet must be prepared.
Who then this Travel to Result would bring
Needs both a Lion's Heart beneath the Wing,
And even more, a Spirit purified
Of Worldly Passion, Malice, Lust, and Pride:

Yea, ev'n of Worldly *Wisdom*, which grows dim
And dark, the nearer it approaches *Him*,
Who to the Spirit's Eye alone reveal'd,
By sacrifice of Wisdom's self unseal'd;
Without which none who reach the Place could bear
To look upon the Glory dwelling there.'

One Night from out the swarming City Gate
Stept holy Bajazyd, to meditate
Alone amid the breathing Fields that lay
In solitary Silence leagues away,
Beneath a Moon and Stars as bright as Day.
And the Saint wondering such a Temple were,
And so lit up, and scarce one worshipper,
A voice from Heav'n amid the stillness said:
'The Royal Road is not for all to tread,
Nor is the Royal Palace for the Rout,
Who, even if they reach it, are shut out.
The Blaze that from my Harim window breaks
With fright the Rabble of the Roadside takes;
And ev'n of those that at my Portal din,
Thousands may knock for one that enters in.'

Thus spoke the Tajidar: and the wing'd Crowd,
That underneath his Word in Silence bow'd,
Clapp'd Acclamation: and their Hearts and Eyes
Were kindled by the Firebrand of the Wise.
They felt their Degradation: they believed
The word that told them how to be retrieved,
And in that glorious Consummation won
Forgot the Cost at which it must be done.
'They only *long'd* to follow: they would go

Whither he led, through Flood, or Fire, or Snow'—
So cried the Multitude. But some there were
Who listen'd with a cold disdainful air,
Content with what they were, or grudging Cost
Of Time or Travel that might all be lost;
These, one by one, came forward, and preferr'd
Unwise Objection: which the wiser Word
Shot with direct Reproof, or subtly round
With Argument and Allegory wound.

The *Pheasant* first would know by what pretence
The Tajidar to that pre-eminence
Was raised—a Bird, but for his lofty Crest
(And such the Pheasant had) like all the Rest—
Who answer'd—'By no Virtue of my own
Sulayman chose me, but by *His* alone:
Not by the Gold and Silver of my Sighs
Made mine, but the free Largess of his Eyes.
Behold the Grace of Allah comes and goes
As to Itself is good: and no one knows
Which way it turns: in that mysterious Court
Not he most finds who furthest travels for't.
For one may crawl upon his knees Life-long,
And yet may never reach, or all go wrong:
Another just arriving at the Place
He toil'd for, and—the Door shut in his Face:
Whereas Another, scarcely gone a Stride,
And suddenly—Behold he is Inside!—
But though the Runner win not, he that *stands*,
No Thorn will turn to Roses in *his* Hands:
Each one must do his best and all endure,
And all endeavour, hoping but not sure.

Heav'n its own Umpire is; its Bidding do,
And Thou perchance shalt be Sulayman's too.'

One day Shah Mahmud, riding with the Wind
A-hunting, left his Retinue behind,
And coming to a River, whose swift Course
Doubled back Game and Dog, and Man and Horse,
Beheld upon the Shore a little Lad
A-fishing, very poor, and Tatter-clad
He was, and weeping as his Heart would break.
So the Great Sultan, for good humour's sake
Pull'd in his Horse a moment, and drew nigh,
And after making his Salam, ask'd why
He wept—weeping, the Sultan said, so sore
As he had never seen one weep before.
The Boy look'd up, and 'O Amir,' he said,
'Sev'n of us are at home, and Father dead,
And Mother left with scarce a Bit of Bread:
And now since Sunrise have I fish'd—and see!
Caught nothing for our Supper—Woe is Me!'
The Sultan lighted from his horse. 'Behold,'
Said he, 'Good Fortune will not be controll'd:
And, since Today yours seems to turn from you,
Suppose we try for once what mine will do,
And we will share alike in all I win.'
So the Shah took, and flung his Fortune in,
The Net; which, cast by the Great Mahmud's Hand,
A hundred glittering Fishes brought to Land.
The Lad look'd up in Wonder—Mahmud smiled
And vaulted into Saddle. But the Child
Ran after—'Nay, Amir, but half the Haul
Is yours by Bargain'—'Nay, Today take all,'

The Sultan cried, and shook his Bridle free—
'But mind—Tomorrow All belongs to Me—'
And so rode off. Next morning at Divan
The Sultan's Mind upon his Bargain ran,
And being somewhat in a mind for sport
Sent for the Lad: who, carried up to Court,
And marching into Royalty's full Blaze
With such a Catch of Fish as yesterday's,
The Sultan call'd and set him by his side,
And asking him, 'What Luck?' The Boy replied,
'*This* is the Luck that follows every Cast,
Since o'er my Net the Sultan's Shadow pass'd.'

Then came *The Nightingale*, from such a Draught
Of Ecstasy that from the Rose he quaff'd
Reeling as drunk, and ever did distil
In exquisite divisions from his Bill
To inflame the Hearts of Men—and thus sang He—
'To me alone, alone, is giv'n the Key
Of Love; of whose whole Mystery possesst,
When I reveal a little to the Rest,
Forthwith Creation listening forsakes
The Reins of Reason, and my Frenzy takes:
Yea, whosoever once has quaint this wine
He leaves unlisten'd David's Song for mine.
In vain do Men for my Divisions strive,
And die themselves making dead Lutes alive:
I hang the Stars with Meshes for Men's Souls:
The Garden underneath my Music rolls.
The long, long Morns that mourn the Rose away
I sit in silence, and on Anguish prey:
But the first Air which the New Year shall breathe

Up to my Boughs of Message from beneath
That in her green Harim my Bride unveils,
My Throat bursts silence and *her* Advent hails,
Who in her crimson Volume registers
The Notes of Him whose Life is lost in hers.
The Rose I love and worship now is here;
If dying, yet reviving, Year by Year;
But that you tell of, all my Life why waste
In vainly searching; or, if found, not taste?'

So with Division infinite and Trill
On would the Nightingale have warbled still,
And all the World have listen'd; but a Note
Of sterner Import check'd the lovesick Throat.

'O watering with thy melodious Tears
Love's Garden, and who dost indeed the Ears
Of men with thy melodious Fingers mould
As David's Finger Iron did of old:
Why not, like David, dedicate thy Dower
Of Song to something better than a Flower?
Empress indeed of Beauty, so they say,
But one whose Empire hardly lasts a Day,
By Insurrection of the Morning's Breath
That made her hurried to Decay and Death:
And while she lasts contented to be seen,
And worshipt, for the Garden's only Queen,
Leaving thee singing on thy Bough forlorn,
Or if she smile on Thee, perhaps in Scorn.'

Like that fond Dervish waiting in the throng
When some World-famous Beauty went along,

Who smiling on the Antic as she pass'd—
Forthwith Staff, Bead and Scrip away he cast,
And grovelling in the Kennel, took to whine
Before her Door among the Dogs and Swine.
Which when she often went unheeding by,
But one day quite as heedless ask'd him—'Why?'—
He told of that one Smile, which, all the Rest
Passing, had kindled Hope within his Breast—
Again she smiled and said, 'O self-beguiled
Poor Wretch, at whom and not on whom I smiled.'

Then came the subtle *Parrot* in a coat
Greener than Greensward, and about his Throat
A Collar ran of sub-sulphureous Gold;
And in his Beak a Sugar-plum he troll'd,
That all his Words with luscious Lisping ran,
And to this Tune—'O cruel Cage, and Man
More iron still who did confine me there,
Who else with him whose Livery I wear
Ere this to his Eternal Fount had been,
And drunk what should have kept me ever-green.
But now I know the Place, and I am free
To go, and all the Wise will follow Me.
Some'—and upon the Nightingale one Eye
He leer'd—'for nothing but the Blossom sigh:
But I am for the luscious Pulp that grows
Where, and for which the Blossom only blows:
And which so long as the Green Tree provides
What better grows along Kaf's dreary Sides?
And what more needful Prophet *there* than He
Who gives me Life to nip it from the Tree?'

To whom the Tajidar—'O thou whose Best
In the green leaf of Paradise is drest,
But whose Neck kindles with a lower Fire—
O slip the collar off of base Desire,
And stand apparell'd in Heav'n's Woof entire!
This Life that hangs so sweet about your Lips
But, spite of all your Khizar, slips and slips,
What is it but itself the coarser Rind
Of the True Life withinside and behind,
Which he shall never never reach unto
Till the gross Shell of Carcase he break through?'

For what said He, that dying Hermit, whom
Your Prophet came to, trailing through the Gloom
His Emerald Vest, and tempted—'Come with Me,
And Live.' The Hermit answered—'Not with Thee.
Two Worlds there are, and *This* was thy Design,
And thou hast got it; but The *Next* is mine;
Whose Fount is *this* life's Death, and to whose Side
Ev'n now I find my Way without a Guide.'

Then like a Sultan glittering in all Rays
Of Jewelry, and deckt with his own Blaze,
The glorious Peacock swept into the Ring:
And, turning slowly that the glorious Thing
Might fill all Eyes with wonder, thus said He.
'Behold, the Secret Artist, making me,
With no one Colour of the skies bedeckt,
But from its Angel's Feathers did select
To make up mine withal, the Gabriel
Of all the Birds: though from my Place I fell
In Eden, when Acquaintance I did make

In those blest days with that Sev'n-headed Snake,
And thence with him, my perfect Beauty marr'd
With these ill Feet, was thrust out and debarr'd.
Little I care for Worldly Fruit or Flower,
Would you restore me to lost Eden's Bower,
But first my Beauty making all complete
With reparation of these ugly Feet.'

'Were it,' 'twas answer'd, 'only to return
To that lost Eden, better far to burn
In Self-abasement up thy pluméd Pride,
And ev'n with lamer feet to creep inside—
But all mistaken you and all like you
That long for that lost Eden as the true;
Fair as it was, still nothing but the shade
And Out-court of the Majesty that made.
That which I point you tow'rd, and which the King
I tell you of broods over with his Wing,
With no deciduous leaf, but with the Rose
Of Spiritual Beauty, smells and glows:
No plot of Earthly Pleasance, but the whole
True Garden of the Universal Soul.'

For so Creation's Master-Jewel fell
From that same Eden: loving which too well,
The Work before the Artist did prefer,
And in the Garden lost the Gardener.
Wherefore one Day about the Garden went
A voice that found him in his false Content,
And like a bitter Sarsar of the North
Shrivell'd the Garden up, and drove him forth

Into the Wilderness: and so the Eye
Of Eden closed on him till by and by.

Then from a Ruin where conceal'd he lay
Watching his buried Gold, and hating Day,
Hooted *The Owl*.—'I tell you, my Delight
Is in the Ruin and the Dead of Night
Where I was born, and where I love to wone
All my Life long, sitting on some cold stone
Away from all your roystering Companies,
In some dark Corner where a Treasure lies;
That, buried by some Miser in the Dark,
Speaks up to me at Midnight like a Spark;
And o'er it like a Talisman I brood,
Companion of the Serpent and the Toad.
What need of other Sovereign, having found,
And keeping as in Prison underground,
One before whom all other Kings bow down,
And with his glittering Heel their Foreheads crown?'

'He that a Miser lives and Miser dies,
At the Last Day what Figure shall he rise?'

A Fellow all his life lived hoarding Gold,
And, dying, hoarded left it. And behold,
One Night his Son saw peering through the House
A Man, with yet the semblance of a Mouse,
Watching a crevice in the Wall—and cried
'My Father?'—'Yes,' the Musulman replied,
'Thy Father!'—'But why watching thus?'—'For fear
Lest any smell my Treasure buried here.'
'But wherefore, Sir, so metamousified?'

18

'Because, my Son, such is the true outside
Of the inner Soul by which I lived and died.'

'Aye,' said *The Partridge*, with his Foot and Bill
Crimson with raking Rubies from the Hill,
And clattering his Spurs—'Wherewith the Ground
I stab,' said he, 'for Rubies, that, when found
I swallow; which, as soon as swallow'd, turn
To Sparks which though my beak and eyes do burn.
Gold, as you say, is but dull Metal dead,
And hanging on the Hoarder's Soul like Lead:
But Rubies that have Blood within, and grown
And nourisht in the Mountain Heart of Stone,
Burn with an inward Light, which they inspire,
And make their Owners Lords of their Desire.'

To whom the Tajidar—'As idly sold
To the quick Pebble as the drowsy Gold,
As dead when sleeping in their mountain mine
As dangerous to Him who makes them shine:
Slavish indeed to do their Lord's Commands,
And slave-like aptest to escape his Hands,
And serve a second Master like the first,
And working all their wonders for the worst.'

Never was Jewel after or before
Like that Sulayman for a Signet wore:
Whereby one Ruby, weighing scarce a grain
Did Sea and Land and all therein constrain,
Yea, ev'n the Winds of Heav'n—made the fierce East
Bear his League-wide Pavilion like a Beast,
Whither he would: yea, the Good Angel held

His subject, and the lower Fiend compell'd.
Till, looking round about him in his pride,
He overtax'd the Fountain that supplied,
Praying that after him no Son of Clay
Should ever touch his Glory. And one Day
Almighty God his Jewel stole away,
And gave it to the Div, who with the Ring
Wore also the Resemblance of the King,
And so for forty days play'd such a Game
As blots Sulayman's forty years with Shame.

Then *The Shah-Falcon*, tossing up his Head
Blink-hooded as it was—'Behold,' he said,
'I am the chosen Comrade of the King,
And perch upon the Fist that wears the Ring;
Born, bred, and nourisht, in the Royal Court,
I take the Royal Name and make the Sport.
And if strict Discipline I undergo
And half my Life am blinded—be it so;
Because the Shah's Companion ill may brook
On aught save Royal Company to look.
And why am I to leave my King, and fare
With all these Rabble Wings I know not where?'—

'O blind indeed'—the Answer was, 'and dark
To any but a vulgar Mortal Mark,
And drunk with Pride of Vassalage to those
Whose Humour like their Kingdom comes and goes;
All Mutability: who one Day please
To give: and next Day what they gave not seize:
Like to the Fire: a dangerous Friend at best,
Which who keeps farthest from does wiseliest.

A certain Shah there was in Days foregone
Who had a lovely Slave he doted on,
And cherish'd as the Apple of his Eye,
Clad gloriously, fed sumptuously, set high,
And never was at Ease were *He* not by,
Who yet, for all this Sunshine, Day by Day
Was seen to wither like a Flower away.
Which, when observing, one without the Veil
Of Favour ask'd the Favourite—'Why so pale
And sad?' thus sadly answer'd the poor Thing—
'No Sun that rises sets until the King,
Whose Archery is famous among Men,
Aims at an Apple on my Head. and when
The stricken Apple splits. and those who stand
Around cry "Lo! the Shah's unerring Hand!"
Then He too laughing asks me "Why so pale
And sorrow-some? as could the Sultan fail,
Who such a master of the Bow confest,
And aiming by the Head that he loves best."'

Then on a sudden swoop'd *The Phoenix* down
As though he wore as well as gave The Crown:
And cried—'I care not, I, to wait on Kings,
Whose crowns are but the Shadow of my Wings!'

'Aye,' was the Answer—'And, pray, how has sped,
On which it lighted, many a mortal Head?'

A certain Sultan dying, his Vizier
In Dream beheld him, and in mortal Fear
Began—'O mighty Shah of Shahs! Thrice-blest'—
But loud the Vision shriek'd and struck its Breast,

And 'Stab me not with empty Title!' cried—
'One only Shah there is, and none beside,
Who from his Throne above for certain Ends
Awhile some Spangle of his Glory lends
To Men on Earth; but calling in again
Exacts a strict account of every Grain.
Sultan I lived, and held the World in scorn:
O better had I glean'd the Field of Corn!
O better had I been a Beggar born,
And for my Throne and Crown, down in the Dust
My living Head had laid where Dead I must!
O wither'd, wither'd, wither'd, be the Wing
Whose overcasting Shadow made me King!'

Then from a Pond, where all day long he kept,
Waddled the dapper *Duck* demure, adept
At infinite Ablution, and precise
In keeping of his Raiment clean and nice.
And 'Sure of all the Race of Birds,' said He,
'None for Religious Purity like Me,
Beyond what strictest Rituals prescribe—
Methinks I am the Saint of all our Tribe,
To whom, by Miracle, the Water, that
I wash in, also makes my Praying-Mat.'

To whom, more angrily than all, replied
The Leader, lashing that religious Pride,
That under ritual Obedience
To outer Law with inner might dispense:
For, fair as all the Feather to be seen,
Could one see *through*, the Maw was not so clean:

But He that made both Maw and Feather too
Would take account of, seeing through and through.

A Shah returning to his Capital,
His subjects drest it forth in Festival,
Thronging with Acclamation Square and Street,
And kneeling flung before his Horse's feet
Jewel and Gold. All which with scarce an Eye
The Sultan superciliously rode by:
Till coming to the public Prison, They
Who dwelt within those grisly Walls, by way
Of Welcome, having neither Pearl nor Gold,
Over the wall chopt Head and Carcase roll'd,
Some almost parcht to Mummy with the Sun,
Some wet with Execution that day done.
At which grim Compliment at last the Shah
Drew Bridle: and amid a wild Hurrah
Of savage Recognition, smiling threw
Silver and Gold among the wretched Crew,
And so rode forward. Whereat of his Train
One wondering that, while others sued in vain
With costly gifts, which carelessly he pass'd,
But smiled at ghastly Welcome like the last;
The Shah made answer—'All that Pearl and Gold
Of ostentatious Welcome only told:
A little with great Clamour from the Store
Of hypocrites who kept at home much more.
But when those sever'd Heads and Trunks I saw—
Save by strict Execution of my Law
They had not parted company; not one
But told my Will not talk'd about, but done.'

Then from a Wood was heard unseen to coo
The *Ring-dove*—'Yúsuf! Yúsuf! Yúsuf! Yú-'
(For thus her sorrow broke her Note in twain,
And, just where broken, took it up again)
'-suf! Yúsuf! Yúsuf! Yúsuf!'—But one Note,
Which still repeating, she made hoarse her throat:

Till checkt—'O You, who with your idle Sighs
Block up the Road of better Enterprise;
Sham Sorrow all, or bad as sham if true,
When once the better thing is come to do;
Beware lest wailing thus you meet his Doom
Who all too long his Darling wept, from whom
You draw the very Name you hold so dear,
And which the World is somewhat tired to hear.'

When Yusuf from his Father's Home was torn,
The Patriarch's Heart was utterly forlorn,
And, like a Pipe with but one stop, his Tongue
With nothing but the name of 'Yusuf' rung.
Then down from Heaven's Branches flew the *Bird
Of Heav'n* and said 'God wearies of that word:
Hast thou not else to do and else to say?'
So Jacob's lips were sealéd from that Day.
But one Night in a Vision, far away
His darling in some alien Field he saw
Binding the Sheaf; and what between the Awe
Of God's Displeasure and the bitter Pass
Of passionate Affection, sigh'd 'Alas—'
And stopp'd—But with the morning Sword of Flame
That oped his Eyes the sterner Angel's came
'For the forbidden Word not utter'd by

Thy Lips was yet sequester'd in that Sigh.'
And the right Passion whose Excess was wrong
Blinded the aged Eyes that wept too long.

And after these came others—arguing,
Enquiring and excusing—some one Thing,
And some another—endless to repeat,
But, in the Main, Sloth, Folly, or Deceit.
Their Souls were to the vulgar Figure cast
Of earthly Victual not of Heavenly Fast.
At last one smaller Bird, of a rare kind,
Of modest Plume and unpresumptuous Mind,
Whisper'd 'O Tajidar, we know indeed
How Thou both knowest, and would'st help our Need;
For thou art wise and holy, and hast been
Behind the Veil, and there The Presence seen.
But we are weak and vain, with little care
Beyond our yearly Nests and daily Fare—
How should we reach the Mountain? and if there
How get so great a Prince to hear our Prayer?
For there, you say, dwells *The Symurgh* alone
In Glory, like Sulayman on his Throne,
And we but Pismires at his feet: can He
Such puny Creatures stoop to hear, or see;
Or hearing, seeing, own us—unakin
As He to Folly, Woe, and Death, and Sin?'—

To whom the Tajidar, whose Voice for those
Bewilder'd ones to full Compassion rose
'O lost so long in exile, you disclaim
The very Fount of Being whence you came,
Cannot be parted from, and, will or no,

Whether for Good or Evil must re-flow!
For look—the Shadows into which the Light
Of his pure Essence down by infinite
Gradation dwindles, which at random play
Through Space in Shape indefinite—one Ray
Of his Creative *Will* into *defined*
Creation quickens: We that swim the Wind,
And they the Flood below, and Man and Beast
That walk between, from Lion to the least
Pismire that creeps along Sulayman's Wall—
Yea, that in which they swim, fly, walk, and crawl—
However near the Fountain Light, or far
Removed, yet *His* authentic Shadows are;
Dead Matter's Self but the dark Residue
Exterminating Glory dwindles to.
A Mystery too fearful in the Crowd
To utter—scarcely to Thyself aloud—
But when in solitary Watch and Prayer
Consider'd: and religiously beware
Lest Thou the Copy with the Type confound;
And *Deity*, with Deity indrown'd,—
For as pure Water into purer Wine
Incorporating shall itself reline
While the dull Drug lies half-resolved below,
With Him and with his Shadows is it so:
The baser Forms, to whatsoever Change
Subject, still vary through their lower Range:
To which the higher even shall decay,
That, letting ooze their better Part away
For Things of Sense and Matter, in the End
Shall merge into the Clay to which they tend.
Unlike to him, who straining through the Bond

Of outward Being for a Life beyond,
While the gross Worldling to *his* Centre clings,
That draws him deeper in, exulting springs
To merge him in the central *Soul* of Things.
And shall not he pass home with other Zest
Who, with full Knowledge, yearns for such a Rest,
Than he, who with his better self at strife,
Drags on the weary Exile call'd *This* Life?—
One, like a child with outstretcht Arms and Face
Upturn'd, anticipates his Sire's Embrace;
The other crouching like a guilty Slave
Till flogg'd to Punishment across the Grave.
And, knowing that *His* glory ill can bear
The unpurged Eye; do thou Thy Breast prepare:
And the mysterious Mirror He set there,
To temper his reflected Image in,
Clear of Distortion, Doubleness, and Sin:
And in thy Conscience understanding *this*,
The *Double* only seems, but The *One is*,
Thyself to Self-annihilation give
That this false Two in that true One may live.
For this I say: if, looking in thy Heart,
Thou for *Self-whole* mistake thy *Shadow-part*,
That Shadow-part indeed into The Sun
Shall melt, but senseless of its Union:
But in that Mirror if with purged eyes
Thy Shadow Thou *for* Shadow recognise,
Then shalt Thou back into thy Centre fall
A conscious Ray of that eternal *All*.'

He ceased, and for awhile Amazement quell'd
The Host, and in the Chain of Silence held:

A Mystery so awful who would dare—
So glorious who would not wish—to share?
So Silence brooded on the feather'd Folk,
Till here and there a timid Murmur broke
From some too poor in honest Confidence,
And then from others of too much Pretence;
Whom both, as each unduly hoped or fear'd,
The Tajidar in answer check'd or cheer'd.

Some said their Hearts were good indeed to go
The Way he pointed out: but they were slow
Of Comprehension, and scarce understood
Their present Evil or the promised Good:
And so, tho' willing to do all they could,
Must not they fall short, or go wholly wrong,
On such mysterious Errand, and so long?
Whom the wise Leader bid but Do their Best
In Hope and Faith, and leave to Him the rest,
For He who fix'd the Race, and knew its Length
And Danger, also knew the Runner's Strength.

Shah Mahmud, absent on an Enterprise,
Ayas, the very Darling of his eyes,
At home under an Evil Eye fell sick,
Then cried the Sultan to a soldier 'Quick!
To Horse! to Horse! without a Moment's Stay,—
The shortest Road with all the Speed you may,—
Or, by the Lord, your Head shall pay for it!'—
Off went the Soldier, plying Spur and Bit—
Over the sandy Desert, over green
Valley, and Mountain, and the Stream between,
Without a Moment's Stop for rest or bait,

Up to the City—to the Palace Gate—
Up to the Presence-Chamber at a Stride—
And Lo! The Sultan at his Darling's side!—
Then thought the Soldier—'I have done my Best,
And yet shall die for it.' The Sultan guess'd
His Thought and smiled. 'Indeed your Best you did,
The nearest Road you knew, and well you rid:
And if *I* knew a shorter, my Excess
Of Knowledge does but justify thy Less.'

And then, with drooping Crest and Feather, came
Others, bow'd down with Penitence and Shame.
They long'd indeed to go; 'but how begin,
Mesh'd and entangled as they were in Sin
Which often-times Repentance of past Wrong
As often broken had but knit more strong?'
Whom the wise Leader bid be of good cheer,
And, conscious of the Fault, dismiss the Fear,
Nor at the very Entrance of the Fray
Their Weapon, ev'n if broken, fling away:
Since Mercy on the broken Branch anew
Would blossom were but each Repentance true.

For did not God his Prophet take to Task?
'Sev'n-times of Thee did Karun Pardon ask;
Which, hadst thou been like Me his Maker—yea,
But present at the Kneading of his Clay
With those twain Elements of Hell and Heav'n,—
One prayer had won what Thou deny'st to Sev'n.'

For like a Child sent with a fluttering Light
To feel his way along a gusty Night

Man walks the World: again and yet again
The Lamp shall be by Fits of Passion slain:
But shall not He who sent him from the Door
Relight the Lamp once more, and yet once more?

When the rebellious Host from Death shall wake
Black with Despair of Judgment, God shall take
Ages of holy Merit from the Count
Of Angels to make up Man's short Amount,
And bid the murmuring Angel gladly spare
Of that which, undiminishing his Share,
Of Bliss, shall rescue Thousands from the Cost
Of Bankruptcy within the Prison lost.

Another Story told how in the Scale
Good Will beyond mere Knowledge would prevail.

In Paradise the Angel Gabriel heard
The Lips of Allah trembling with the Word
Of perfect Acceptation: and he thought
'Some perfect Faith such perfect Answer wrought,
But whose?'—And therewith slipping from the Crypt
Of Sidra, through the Angel-ranks he slipt
Watching what Lip yet trembled with the Shot
That so had hit the Mark—but found it not.
Then, in a Glance to Earth, he threaded through
Mosque, Palace, Cell and Cottage of the True
Belief—in vain; so back to Heaven went
And—Allah's Lips still trembling with assent!
Then the tenacious Angel once again
Threaded the Ranks of Heav'n and Earth—in vain—

Till, once again return'd to Paradise,
There, looking into God's, the Angel's Eyes
Beheld the Prayer that brought that Benison
Rising like Incense from the Lips of one
Who to an Idol bowed—as best he knew
Under that False God worshipping the True.

And then came others whom the summons found
Not wholly sick indeed, but far from sound:
Whose light inconstant Soul alternate flew
From Saint to Sinner, and to both untrue;
Who like a niggard Tailor, tried to match
Truth's single Garment with a worldly Patch.
A dangerous Game; for, striving to adjust
The hesitating Scale of either Lust,
That which had least within it upward flew,
And still the weightier to the Earth down drew,
And, while suspended between Rise and Fall,
Apt with a shaking Hand to forfeit all.

There was a Queen of Egypt like the Bride
Of Night, Full-moon-faced and Canopus-eyed,
Whom one among the meanest of her Crowd
Loved—and she knew it (for he loved aloud),
And sent for him, and said 'Thou lov'st thy Queen:
Now therefore Thou hast this to choose between:
Fly for thy Life: or for this one night Wed
Thy Queen, and with the Sunrise lose thy Head.'
He paused—he turn'd to fly—she struck him dead.
'For had he truly loved his Queen,' said She,
'He would at once have giv'n his Life for me,

And Life and Wife had carried: but he lied;
And loving only Life, has justly died.'

And then came one who having clear'd his Throat
With sanctimonious Sweetness in his Note
Thus lisp'd—'Behold I languish from the first
With passionate and unrequited Thirst
Of Love for more than any mortal Bird.
Therefore have I withdrawn me from the Herd
To pine in Solitude. But Thou at last
Hast drawn a line across the dreary Past,
And sure I am by Foretaste that the Wine
I long'd for, and Thou tell'st of, shall be mine.'

But he was sternly checkt. 'I tell thee this:
Such Boast is no Assurance of such Bliss:
Thou canst not even fill the sail of Prayer
Unless from *Him* breathe that authentic Air
That shall lift up the Curtain that divides
His Lover from the Harim where *He* hides—
And the Fulfilment of thy Vows must be,
Not from thy Love for Him, but His for Thee.'

The third night after Bajazyd had died,
One saw him, in a dream, at his Bedside,
And said, 'Thou Bajazyd? Tell me O Pyr,
How fared it there with Munkar and Nakyr?'
And Bajazyd replied, 'When from the Grave
They met me rising, and "If Allah's slave"
Ask'd me, "or collar'd with the Chain of Hell?"
I said "Not I but God alone can tell:
My Passion for his service were but fond

Ambition had not He approved the Bond:
Had He not round my neck the Collar thrown
And told me in the Number of his own;
And that He only knew. What signifies
A hundred Years of Prayer if none replies?"'

'But,' said Another, 'then shall none the Seal
Of Acceptation on his Forehead feel
Ere the Grave yield them on the other Side
Where all is settled?'

    But the Chief replied—
'Enough for us to know that who is meet
Shall enter, and with unreprovéd Feet,
(Ev'n as he might upon the Waters walk)
The Presence-room, and in the Presence talk
With such unbridled Licence as shall seem
To the Uninitiated to blaspheme.'

Just as another Holy Spirit fled,
The Skies above him burst into a Bed
Of Angels looking down and singing clear
'Nightingale! Nightingale! thy Rose is here!'
And yet, the Door wide open to that Bliss,
As some hot Lover slights a scanty Kiss,
The Saint cried 'All I sigh'd for come to *this?*
I who lifelong have struggled, Lord, to be
Not of thy Angels one, but one with Thee!'

Others were sure that all he said was true:
They were extremely wicked, that they knew:
And much they long'd to go at once—but some,

They said, so unexpectedly had come
Leaving their Nests half-built—in bad Repair—
With Children in—Themselves about to pair—
'Might he not choose a better Season—nay,
Better perhaps a Year or Two's Delay,
Till all was settled, and themselves more stout
And strong to carry their Repentance out—
And then'—

     'And then, the same or like Excuse,
With harden'd Heart and Resolution loose
With dallying: and old Age itself engaged
Still to shirk that which shirking we have aged:
And so with Self-delusion, till, too late,
Death upon all Repentance shuts the Gate;
Or some fierce blow compels the Way to choose,
And forced Repentance half its Virtue lose.'

As of an aged Indian King they tell
Who, when his Empire with his Army fell
Under young Mahmud's Sword of Wrath, was sent
At sunset to the Conqueror in his Tent;
But, ere the old King's silver head could reach
The Ground, was lifted up—with kindly Speech,
And with so holy Mercy reassured,
That, after due Persuasion, he abjured
His idols, sate upon Mahmud's Divan,
And took the Name and Faith of Musulman.
But when the Night fell, in his Tent alone
The poor old King was heard to weep and groan
And smite his Bosom; which, when Mahmud knew,
He went to him and said 'Lo, if Thou rue

Thy lost Dominion, Thou shalt wear the Ring
Of thrice as large a Realm.' But the dark King
Still wept, and Ashes on his Forehead threw
And cried 'Not for my Kingdom lost I rue:
But thinking how at the Last Day, will stand
The Prophet with *The Volume* in his Hand,
And ask of me "How was't that, in thy Day
Of Glory, Thou didst turn from Me and slay
My People; but soon as thy Infidel
Before my True Believers' Army fell
Like Corn before the Reaper—thou didst own
His Sword who scoutedst *Me*." Of seed so sown
What profitable Harvest should be grown?'

Then after cheering others who delay'd,
Not of the Road but of Themselves afraid,
The Tajidar the Troop of those address'd,
Whose uncomplying Attitude confess'd
Their Souls entangled in the old Deceit,
And hankering still after forbidden Meat—
'O ye who so long feeding on the Husk
Forgo the Fruit, and doting on the Dusk
Of the false Dawn, are blinded to the True:
That in the Maidan of this World pursue
The Golden Ball which, driven to the Goal,
Wins the World's Game but loses your own Soul:
Or like to Children after Bubbles run
That still elude your Fingers; or, if won,
Burst in Derision at your Touch; all thin
Glitter without, and empty Wind within.
So as a prosperous Worldling on the Bed
Of Death—"Behold, I am as one," he said,

"Who all my Life long have been measuring Wind,
And, dying, now leave even that behind"—
This World's a Nest in which the Cockatrice
Is warm'd and hatcht of Vanity and Vice:
A false Bazaar whose Wares are all a lie,
Or never worth the Price at which you buy:
A many-headed Monster that, supplied
The faster, faster is unsatisfied;
So as one, hearing a rich Fool one day
To God for yet one other Blessing pray,
Bid him no longer bounteous Heaven tire
For Life to feed, but Death to quench, the Fire.
And what are all the Vanities and Wiles
In which the false World decks herself and smiles
To draw Men down into her harlot Lap?
Lusts of the Flesh that Soul and Body sap,
And, melting Soul down into carnal Lust,
Ev'n that for which 'tis sacrificed disgust:
Or Lust of worldly Glory—hollow more
Than the Drum beaten at the Sultan's Door,
And fluctuating with the Breath of Man
As the Vain Banner flapping in the Van.
And Lust of Gold—perhaps of Lusts the worst;
The mis-created Idol most accurst
That between Man and Him who made him stands:
The Felon that with suicidal hands
He sweats to dig and rescue from his Grave,
And sets at large to make Himself its Slave.

'For lo, to what worse than oblivion gone
Are some the cozening World most doted on.
Pharaoh tried *Glory*: and his Chariots drown'd:

Karun with all his Gold went underground:
Down toppled Nembroth with his airy Stair:
Schedad among his Roses lived—but *where?*

'And as the World upon her victims feeds
So She herself goes down the Way she leads.
For all her false allurements are the Threads
The Spider from her Entrail spins, and spreads
For Home and hunting-ground: And by and by
Darts at due Signal on the tangled Fly,
Seizes, dis-wings, and drains the Life, and leaves
The swinging Carcase, and forthwith re-weaves
Her Web: each Victim adding to the store
Of poison'd Entrail to entangle more.
And so She bloats in Glory: till one Day
The Master of the House, passing that way,
Perceives, and with one flourish of his Broom
Of Web and Fly and Spider clears the Room.

'Behold, dropt through the Gate of Mortal Birth,
The Knightly Soul alights from Heav'n on Earth;
Begins his Race, but scarce the Saddle feels,
When a foul Imp up from the distance steals,
And, double as he will, about his Heels
Closer and ever closer circling creeps,
Then, half-invited, on the Saddle leaps,
Clings round the Rider, and, once there, in vain
The strongest strives to thrust him off again.
In Childhood just peeps up the Blade of Ill,
That Youth to Lust rears, Fury, and Self-will:
And, as Man cools to sensual Desire,
Ambition catches with as fierce a Fire;

Until Old Age sends him with one last Lust
Of Gold, to keep it where he found—in Dust.
Life at both ends so feeble and constrain'd
How should that Imp of Sin be slain or chain'd?

'And woe to him who feeds the hateful Beast
That of his Feeder makes an after-feast!
We know the Wolf: by Strategem and Force
Can hunt the Tiger down: but what Resource
Against the Plague we heedless hatch within,
Then, growing, pamper into full-blown Sin
With the Soul's self: ev'n, as the wise man said,
Feeding the very Devil with God's own Bread;
Until the Lord his Largess misapplied
Resent, and drive us wholly from his Side?

'For should the Greyhound whom a Sultan fed,
And by a jewell'd String a-hunting led,
Turned by the Way to gnaw some nasty Thing
And snarl at Him who twitch'd the silken String,
Would not his Lord soon weary of Dispute,
And turn adrift the incorrigible Brute?

'Nay, would one follow, and without a Chain,
The only Master truly worth the Pain,
One must beware lest, growing over-fond
Of even Life's more consecrated Bond,
We clog our Footsteps to the World beyond.
Like that old Arab Chieftain, who confess'd
His soul by two too Darling Things possess'd—
That only Son of his: and that one Colt
Descended from the Prophet's Thunderbolt.

"And I might well bestow the last," he said,
"On him who brought me Word the Boy was dead."
'And if so vain the glittering Fish we get,
How doubly vain to dote upon the Net,
Call'd Life, that draws them, patching up this thin
Tissue of Breathing out and Breathing in,
And so by husbanding each wretched Thread
Spin out Death's very terror that we dread—
For as the Raindrop from the sphere of God
Dropt for a while into the Mortal Clod
So little makes of its allotted Time
Back to its Heav'n itself to re-sublime,
That it but serves to saturate its Clay
With Bitterness that will not pass away.'

One day the Prophet on a River Bank,
Dipping his Lips into the Channel, drank
A Draught as sweet as Honey. Then there came
One who an earthen Pitcher from the same
Drew up, and drank: and after some short stay
Under the Shadow, rose and went his Way.
Leaving his earthen Bowl. In which, anew
Thirsting, the Prophet from the River drew,
And drank from: but the Water that came up
Sweet from the Stream. drank bitter from the Cup.
At which the Prophet in a still Surprise
For Answer turning up to Heav'n his Eyes,
The Vessel's Earthen Lips with Answer ran—
'The Clay that I am made of once was Man,
Who dying, and resolved into the same
Obliterated Earth from which he came
Was for the Potter dug, and chased in turn

Through long Vicissitude of Bowl and Urn:
But howsoever moulded, still the Pain
Of that first mortal Anguish would retain,
And cast, and re-cast, for a Thousand years
Would turn the sweetest Water into Tears.'

And after Death?—that, shirk it as we may,
Will come, and with it bring its After-Day—

For ev'n as Yusuf (when his Brotherhood
Came up from Egypt to buy Corn, and stood
Before their Brother in his lofty Place,
Nor knew him, for a Veil before his Face)
Struck on his Mystic Cup, which straightway then
Rung out their Story to those guilty Ten:—
Not to *them* only, but to every one;
Whatever he have said and thought and done,
Unburied with the Body shall fly up,
And gather into Heav'n's inverted Cup,
Which, stricken by God's Finger, shall tell all
The Story whereby we must stand or fall.
And though we walk this World as if behind
There were no Judgement, or the Judge half-blind,
Beware, for He with whom we have to do
Outsees the Lynx, outlives the Phoenix too—

So Sultan Mahmud, coming Face to Face
With mightier numbrs of the swarthy Race,
Vow'd that if God to him the battle gave,
God's Dervish People all the Spoil should have.
And God the Battle gave him; and the Fruit
Of a great Conquest coming to compute,

A Murmur through the Sultan's Army stirr'd
Lest, ill committed to one hasty Word,
The Shah should squander on an idle Brood
What should be theirs who earn'd it with their Blood,
Or go to fill the Coffers of the State.
So Mahmud's Soul began to hesitate:
Till looking round in Doubt from side to side
A raving Zealot in the Press he spied,
And call'd and had him brought before his Face,
And, telling, bid him arbitrate the case.
Who, having listen'd, said—'The Thing is plain:
If Thou and God should never have again
To deal together, rob him of his share:
But if perchance you should—why then Beware!'

So spake the Tajidar: but Fear and Doubt
Among the Birds in Whispers went about:
Great was their Need: and Succour to be sought
At any Risk: at any Ransom bought:
But such a Monarch—greater than Mahmud
The Great Himself! Why how should he be woo'd
To listen to them? they too have come
O So suddenly, and unprepared from home
With any Gold, or Jewel, or rich Thing
To carry with them to so great a King—
Poor Creatures! with the old and carnal Blind,
Spite of all said, so thick upon the Mind,
Devising how they might ingratiate
Access, as to some earthly Potentate.

'Let him that with this Monarch would engage
Bring the Gold Dust of a long Pilgrimage:

The Ruby of a bleeding Heart, whose Sighs
Breathe more than Amber-incense as it dies;
And while in naked Beggary he stands
Hope for the Robe of Honour from his Hands.'
And, as no gift this Sovereign receives
Save the mere Soul and Self of him who gives,
So let that Soul for other none Reward
Look than the Presence of its Sovereign Lord.'
And as his Hearers seem'd to estimate
Their Scale of Glory from Mahmud the Great,
A simple Story of the Sultan told
How best a subject with his Shah made bold—

One night Shah Mahmud who had been of late
Somewhat distemper'd with Affairs of State
Stroll'd through the Streets disguised, as wont to do—
And, coming to the Baths, there on the Flue
Saw the poor Fellow who the Furnace fed
Sitting beside his Water-jug and Bread.
Mahmud stept in—sat down—unask'd took up
And tasted of the untasted Loaf and Cup,
Saying within himself, 'Grudge but a bit,
And, by the Lord, your Head shall pay for it!'
So having rested, warm'd and satisfied
Himself without a Word on either side,
At last the wayward Sultan rose to go.
And then at last his Host broke silence—'So?—
Art satisfied? Well, Brother, any Day
Or Night, remember, when you come this Way
And want a bit of Provender—why, you
Are welcome, and if not—why, welcome too.'—

The Sultan was so tickled with the whim
Of this quaint Entertainment and of him
Who offer'd it, that many a Night again
Stoker and Shah forgather'd in that Vein—
Till, the poor Fellow having stood the Test
Of true Good-fellowship, Mahmud confess'd
One Night the Sultan that had been his Guest:
And in requital of the scanty Dole
The Poor Man offer'd with so large a soul,
Bid him ask any Largess that he would
A Throne—if he *would* have it, so he *should*.
The Poor Man kiss'd the Dust, and 'All,' said he,
'I ask is what and where I am to be;
If but the Shah from time to time will come
As now and see me in the lowly Home
His presence makes a palace, and my own
Poor Flue more royal than another's Throne.'

So said the cheery Tale: and, as they heard,
Again the Heart beneath the Feather stirr'd:
Again forgot the Danger and the Woes
Of the long Travel in its glorious Close:—
'Here truly all was Poverty, Despair
And miserable Banishment—but there
That more than Mahmud, for no more than Prayer
Who would restore them to their ancient Place,
And round their Shoulders fling his Robe of Grace.'
They clapp'd their Wings, on Fire to be assay'd
And prove of what true Metal they were made,
Although defaced, and wanting the true Ring
And Superscription of their rightful King.

'The Road! The Road!' in countless voices cried
The Host—'The Road! and who shall be our Guide?'
And they themselves 'The Tajidar!' replied:
Yet to make doubly certain that the Voice
Of Heav'n according with the People's Choice,
Lots should be drawn; and He on whom should light
Heav'n's Hand—they swore to follow him outright.
This settled, and once more the Hubbub quell'd,
Once more Suspense the Host in Silence held,
While, Tribe by Tribe, the Birds their fortune drew;
And Lo! upon the Tajidar it flew.
Then rising up again in wide and high
Circumference of wings that mesh'd the sky
'The Tajidar! The Tajidar!' they cry—
'The Tajidar! The Tajidar!' with Him
Was Heav'n, and They would follow Life and Limb!
Then, once more fluttering to their Places down,
Upon his Head they set the Royal Crown
As Khalif of their Khalif so long lost,
And Captain of his now repentant Host;
And setting him on high, and Silence call'd,
The Tajidar, in Pulpit-throne install'd,
His Voice into a Trumpet-tongue so clear
As all the winged Multitude should hear
Raised, to proclaim the Order and Array
Of March; which, many as it frighten'd—yea,
The Heart of Multitudes at outset broke,
Yet for due Preparation must be spoke.

—A Road indeed that never Wing before
Flew, nor Foot trod, nor Heart imagined—o'er
Waterless Deserts—Waters where no Shore—

Valleys comprising cloud-high Mountains: these
Again their Valleys deeper than the Seas:
Whose Dust all Adders, and whose vapour Fire:
Where all once hostile Elements conspire
To set the Soul against herself, and tear
Courage to Terror—Hope into Despair,
And Madness; Terrors, Trials, to make stray
Or Stop where Death to wander or delay:
Where when half dead with Famine, Toil, and Heat,
'Twas Death indeed to rest, or drink, or eat.
A Road still waxing in Self-sacrifice
As it went on: still ringing with the Cries
And Groans of Those who had not yet prevail'd,
And bleaching with the Bones of those who fail'd:
Where, almost all withstood, perhaps to earn
Nothing: and, earning, never to return.—
And first the *VALE OF SEARCH:* an endless Maze,
Branching into innumerable Ways
All courting Entrance: but one right: and this
Beset with Pitfall, Gulf, and Precipice,
Where Dust is Embers, Air a fiery Sleet,
Through which with blinded Eyes and bleeding Feet
The Pilgrim stumbles, with Hyena's Howl
Around, and hissing Snake, and deadly Ghoul,
Whose Prey he falls if tempted but to droop,
Or if to wander famish'd from the Troop
For fruit that falls to ashes in the Hand,
Water that reacht recedes into the Sand.
The only word is 'Forward!' Guide in sight,
After him, swerving neither left nor right,
Thyself for thine own Victual by Day,
At night thine own Self's Caravanserai.

Till suddenly, perhaps when most subdued
And desperate, the Heart shall be renew'd
When deep in utter Darkness, by one Gleam
Of Glory from the far remote *Harim*,
That, with a scarcely conscious Shock of Change,
Shall light the Pilgrim toward the Mountain Range
Of KNOWLEDGE: where, if stronger and more pure
The Light and Air, yet harder to endure;
And if, perhaps, the Footing more secure,
Harder to keep up with a nimble Guide,
Less from lost Road than insufficient Stride—
Yet tempted still by false Shows from the Track,
And by false Voices call'd aside or back,
Which echo from the Bosom, as if won
The Journey's End when only just begun,
And not a Mountain Peak with Toil attain'd
But shows a top yet higher to be gain'd.
Wherefore still Forward, Forward! Love that fired
Thee first to search, by Search so re-inspired
As that the Spirit shall the carnal Load
Burn up, and double wing Thee on the Road;
That wert thou knocking at the very Door
Of Heav'n, thou still would'st cry for More, More, More!

Till loom in sight Kaf's Mountain Peak ashroud
In Mist—uncertain yet Mountain or Cloud,
But where the Pilgrim 'gins to hear the Tide
Of that one Sea in which the Sev'n subside;
And not the Sev'n Seas only: but the sev'n
And self-enfolded Spheres of Earth and Heav'n—
Yea, the Two Worlds, that now as Pictures sleep
Upon its Surface—but when once the Deep

From its long Slumber 'gins to heave and sway—
Under the Tempest shall be swept away
With all their Phases and Phenomena:
Not senseless Matter only, but combined
With Life in all Varieties of Kind;
Yea, ev'n the abstract Forms that Space and Time
Men call, and Weal and Woe, Virtue and Crime,
And all the several Creeds like those who fell
Before them, Musulman and Infidel
Shall from the Face of Being melt away,
Cancell'd and swept as Dreams before the Day.
So hast thou seen the Astrologer prepare
His mystic Table smooth of sand, and there
Inscribe his mystic figures, Square, and Trine,
Circle and Pentagram, and heavenly Sign
Of Star and Planet: from whose Set and Rise,
Meeting and Difference, he prophesies;
And, having done it, with his Finger clean
Obliterates as never they had been.

Such is when reacht the Table Land of One
And *Wonder:* blazing with so fierce a Sun
Of Unity that blinds while it reveals
The Universe that to a Point congeals,
So, stunn'd with utter Revelation, reels
The Pilgrim, when that *Double*-seeming House,
Against whose Beams he long had chafed his Brows,
Crumbles and cracks before that Sea, whose near
And nearer Voice now overwhelms his Ear.
Till blinded, deafen'd, madden'd, drunk with doubt
Of all within Himself as all without,
Nay, whether a *Without* there be, or not,

Or a *Within* that doubts: and if, then what?—
Ev'n so shall the bewilder'd Pilgrim seem
When nearest waking deepliest in Dream,
And darkest next to Dawn; and lost what had
When *All* is found: and just when sane quite Mad—
As one that having found the Key once more
Returns, and Lo! he cannot find the Door
He stumbles over—So the Pilgrim stands
A moment on the Threshold—with raised Hands
Calls to the eternal Saki for one Draught
Of Light from the One Essence: which when quaff'd,
He plunges headlong in: and all is well
With him who never more returns to tell.
Such being then the Race and such the Goal,
Judge if you must not Body both and Soul
With Meditation, Watch and Fast prepare.
For he that wastes his body to a Hair
Shall seize the Locks of Truth: and He that prays
Good Angels in their Ministry waylays:
And the Midnightly Watcher in the Folds
Of his own Darkness God Almighty holds.
He that would prosper here must from him strip
The World, and take the Dervish Gown and Scrip:
And as he goes must gather from all Sides
Irrelevant Ambitions, Lusts and Prides,
Glory and Gold, and sensual Desire,
Whereof to build the fundamental Pyre
Of Self-annihilation: and cast in
All old Relations and Regards of Kin
And Country: and, the Pile with this perplext
World platform'd, from the Fables of the Next
Raise it tow'rd Culmination, with the torn

Rags and Integuments of Creeds out-worn;
And top the giddy Summit with the Scroll
Of *Reason* that in dingy Smoke shall roll
Over the true Self-sacrifice of Soul:
(For such a Prayer was his—'O God, do Thou
With all my Wealth in the other World endow
My Friends: and with my Wealth in *this* my Foes,
Till bankrupt in *thy* Riches I repose!')
Then, all the Pile completed of the Pelf
Of either World—at last throw on *Thyself*,
And with the torch of Self-negation fire;
And ever as the Flames rise high and higher,
With Cries of agonising Glory still
All of that *Self* burn up that burn up will,
Leaving the Phoenix that no Fire can slay
To spring from its own Ashes kindled—nay,
Itself an inextinguishable Spark
Of Being, *now* beneath Earth-ashes dark,
Transcending these, at last *Itself* transcends
And with the One Eternal Essence blends.

The Moths had long been exiled from the Flame
They worship: so to solemn Council came,
And voted *One* of them by Lot be sent
To find their Idol. One was chosen: went.
And after a long Circuit in sheer Gloom,
Seeing, he thought, the TAPER in a Room
Flew back at once to say so. But the chief
Of *Mothistan* slighted so slight Belief,
And sent another Messenger, who flew
Up to the House, in at the window, through
The Flame itself; and back the Message brings,

With yet no sign of Conflict on his wings.
Then went a Third, and spurr'd with true Desire,
Plunging at once into the sacred Fire,
Folded his Wings within, till he became
One Colour and one Substance with the Flame.
He only knew the Flame who in it burn'd;
And only He could tell who ne'er to tell return'd.

After declaring what of this declared
Must be, that all who went should be prepared,
From his high Station ceased the Tajidar—
And lo! the Terrors that, when told afar,
Seem'd but as Shadows of a Noonday Sun,
Now that the talkt-of Thing was to be *done*,
Lengthening into those of closing Day
Strode into utter Darkness: and Dismay
Like Night on the husht Sea of Feathers lay,
Late so elate—'So terrible a Track!
Endless—or, ending, never to come back!—
Never to Country, Family, or Friend!'—
In sooth no easy Bow for Birds to bend!—
Even while he spoke, how many Wings and Crests
Had slunk away to distant Woods and Nests;
Others again in Preparation spent
What little Strength they had, and never went:
And others, after preparation due—
When up the Veil of that first Valley drew
From whose waste Wilderness of Darkness blew
A Sarsar, whether edged of Flames or Snows,
That through from Root to Tip their Feathers froze—
Up went a Multitude that overhead
A moment darken'd, then on all sides fled,

Dwindling the World-assembled Caravan
To less than half the Number that began.
Of those who fled not, some in Dread and Doubt
Sat without stirring: others who set out
With frothy Force, or stupidly resign'd,
Before a League, flew off or fell behind.
And howsoever the more Brave and Strong
In Courage, Wing, or Wisdom push'd along,
Yet League by League the Road was thicklier spread
By the fast falling Foliage of the Dead:
Some spent with Travel over Wave and Ground;
Scorcht, frozen, dead for Drought, or drinking drown'd.
Famisht, or poison'd with the Food when found:
By Weariness, or Hunger, or Affright
Seduced to stop or stray, become the Bite
Of Tiger howling round or hissing Snake,
Or Crocodile that eyed them from the Lake:
Or raving Mad, or in despair Self-slain:
Or slaying one another for a Grain:—

Till of the mighty Host that fledged the Dome
Of Heav'n and Floor of Earth on leaving Home,
A Handful reach'd and scrambled up the Knees
Of Kaf whose Feet dip in the Seven Seas;
And of the few that up his Forest-sides
Of Light and Darkness where *The Presence* hides,
But *Thirty*—thirty desperate draggled Things,
Half-dead, with scarce a Feather on their Wings,
Stunn'd, blinded, deafen'd with the Crash and Craze
Of Rock and Sea collapsing in a Blaze
That struck the Sun to Cinder—fell upon
The Threshold of the Everlasting *One*,

With but enough of Life in each to cry,
On THAT which all absorb'd—
And suddenly
Forth flash'd a winged Harbinger of Flame
And Tongue of Fire, and 'Who?' and 'Whence they came?'
And 'Why?' demanded. And the Tajidar
For all the Thirty answer'd him—'We are
Those Fractions of the Sum of Being, far
Dis-spent and foul disfigured, that once more
Strike for Admission at the Treasury Door.'
To whom the Angel answer'd—'Know ye not
That He you seek recks little who or what
Of Quantity and Kind—himself the Fount
Of Being Universal needs no Count
Of all the Drops o'erflowing from his Urn,
In what Degree they issue or return?'

Then cried the Spokesman, 'Be it even so:
Let us but see the Fount from which we flow,
'And, seeing, lose Ourselves therein!' and, Lo!
Before the Word was utter'd, or the Tongue
Of Fire replied, or Portal open flung.
They were *within*—they were before the *Throne*,
Before the Majesty that sat thereon,
But wrapt in so insufferable a Blaze
Of Glory as beat down their baffled Gaze.
Which, downward dropping, fell upon a Scroll
That, Lightning-like, flash'd back on each the whole
Past half-forgotten Story of his Soul:
Like that which Yusuf in his Glory gave
His Brethren as some Writing he would have
Interpreted; and at a Glance, behold

Their own Indenture for their Brother sold!
And so with these poor Thirty: who, abasht
In Memory all laid bare and Conscience lasht,
By full Confession and Self-loathing flung
The Rags of carnal Self that round them clung;
And, their old selves self-knowledged and self-loathed,
And in the Soul's Integrity re-clothed,
Once more they ventured from the Dust to raise
Their Eyes—up to the Throne—into the Blaze,
And in the Centre of the Glory there
Beheld the Figure of—*Themselves*—as 'twere
Transfigured—looking to Themselves, beheld
The Figure on the Throne en-miracled,
Until their Eyes themselves and That between
Did hesitate which *Sëer* was, which *Seen*;
They That, That They: Another, yet the Same:
Dividual, yet One: from whom there came
A Voice of awful Answer, scarce discern'd
From *which* to Aspiration *whose* return'd
They scarcely knew; as when some Man apart
Answers aloud the Question in his Heart—
'The Sun of my Perfection is a Glass
Wherein from *Seeing* into *Being* pass
All who, reflecting as reflected see
Themselves in Me, and Me in Them: not Me,
But all of Me that a contracted Eye
Is comprehensive of Infinity:
Nor yet *Themselves*: no Selves, but of The All
Fractions, from which they split and whither fall.
As Water lifted from the Deep, again
Falls back in individual Drops of Rain
Then melts into the Universal Main.

All you have been, and seen, and done, and thought,
Not *You* but *I*, have seen and been and wrought:
I was the Sin that from Myself rebell'd:
I the Remorse that tow'rd Myself compell'd:
I was the Tajidar who led the Track:
I was the little Briar that pull'd you back:
Sin and Contrition—Retribution owed,
And cancell'd—Pilgrim, Pilgrimage, and Road,
Was but Myself toward Myself: and Your
Arrival but *Myself* at my own Door:
Who in your Fraction of Myself behold
Myself within the Mirror Myself hold
To see Myself in, and each part of Me
That sees himself, though drown'd, shall ever see.
Come you lost Atoms to your Centre draw,
And *be* the Eternal Mirror that you saw:
Rays that have wander'd into Darkness wide
Return, and back into your Sun subside.'—

This was the Parliament of Birds: and this
The Story of the Host who went amiss,
And of the Few that better Upshot found;
Which being now recounted, Lo, the Ground
Of Speech fails underfoot: But this to tell—
Their Road is thine—Follow—and Fare thee well.

BIBLIOBAZAAR

The essential book market!

Did you know that you can get any of our titles in large print?

Did you know that we have an ever-growing collection of books in many languages?

Order online:
www.bibliobazaar.com

Find all of your favorite classic books!

Stay up to date with the latest government reports!

At BiblioBazaar, we aim to make knowledge more accessible by making thousands of titles available to you- *quickly and affordably*.

Contact us:
BiblioBazaar
PO Box 21206
Charleston, SC 29413